I AM Creating My Own Financial Freedom: The Story

by
Barry Thomas Bechta

UNCONDITIONAL LOVE BOOKS

Redefining, Guiding, and Inspiring Humanity's Connection to the Creative Power within.

I AM Creating My Own Financial Freedom: The Story
by
Barry Thomas Bechta

Library and Archives Canada Cataloguing in Publication

Bechta, Barry Thomas, 1968-
   I am creating my own financial freedom : the story /
by Barry Thomas Bechta.

ISBN 978-0-9813485-2-0

   1. Finance, Personal. 2. Financial security.
3. Wealth. I. Title.

HG179.B4263 2009   332.024'01   C2009-906821-4

Publisher's Note
This publication is designed to provide accurate and authoritative information in regard to the subject matter covered. It is sold with the understanding that the author/publisher is not engaged in rendering psychological, legal, or other professional service. If advice or other assistance is required in those areas, the services of a competent professional should be sought.

I AM
Creating My
Own   Financial
Freedom: The Story

I Had A Dream For My Family

I Believed It Before I Could See It

Now I Live This Dream With My Family

ACKNOWLEDGEMENTS

Thank You God

Thank You Binah

Thank You Anthony

Thank You Zach

Thank You Clare and Ellen

Thank You Melinda, Paul, Sydney, and Gryphon

Thank You Stephen, Margaret, Gabe, and Sam

Thank You Rachel, Neil, and Miracle

Thank You Kimiko, Ernie and Inga, Uschi, Walter, and Peter

Thank You Esther and Jerry and ABRAHAM, Neale, Eckhart, Wayne, Louise, Mark, Robert, Jack, Alan, Louise, Richard, John and Jan, Prince, Michael, Sandra, Terry, Marc, Shakti, Lenedra, Ernest, Iyanla, Deepak, Jamie, Napoleon, Oprah, Anthony, Joe, Pat, Helen and Thetford, Brock and Wilma.

And I Truly Thank YOU.

TO THE READER

I love money.

I feel this way today, but I have not always felt this way about money.

I have enjoyed money. I have hated money. I have been lost with money. I have been lost without money. I have had many experiences with money one can have from debt to abundance, from generosity to animosity, and from pain to pleasure.

All the while, I wanted a better working relationship with money.

The ideas we hold about money take us wherever those ideas lead to. Our ideas can lead us to less money, or our ideas can lead us to more money. Either way we get whatever we have in life because of the ideas we hold and work with. Many times, we hold and work with ideas we do not even know we have.

If you change nothing, nothing changes.

If you change something, something changes.

If you Consciously Choose what you are changing, then your changes become Conscious.

Follow and enjoy the journey in this book. This book is a mirror to your life. The story is about others, but the journey is yours if you Consciously Choose to take it.

The ideas contained in this story are very simple. Please don't let that simplicity fool you, for these ideas are very powerful too.

Build Joyful Financial Freedom*,*
Barry Thomas Bechta

TABLE OF CONTENTS

WHAT'S IT GONNA TAKE?

The door bell rang the same cheerful tone it rings for everyone, but Bill Right did not hear it. He could have heard the bell's joy had he been in a better feeling place.

Alas, this morning he was stuck in his own thoughts of disconnection.

"What's it gonna take, Bill?" Jonathan, the owner of the coffee shop asked from behind the counter.

"That's the question, isn't it?" Bill replied.

"I meant coffee."

"I didn't."

"I know."

Bill continued, "Have you ever just wished you could figure it out?"

"Many times."

"Me too."

"You'll figure it out."

"Thanks for the vote of confidence." Bill said, "My problem is ..."

"Let me guess. Love or money or health."

"Money."

"It's usually one of the three."

"Really?"

"Owning a coffee shop, you hear them all."

"So what do you suggest?"

"Depends."

"On what?"

"Where you want to get to."

"I want to get out of this hole I am in."

"That's where you are."

"What?"

"I asked where do you want to get to?"

"I want to get to financial freedom."

"Would you like the usual as you go towards financial freedom today?"

"Yeah." Bill said absentmindedly.

"No. No. No you don't."

"Pardon?"

"The usual is only going to take you to the same place you already are."

"Are we talking about coffee?"

"No."

"Try this instead." Jonathan rung up a drink and called out an order, "One 77 Special."

Now when Jonathan called out the 77 Special, he was animated as he said it. His arms waved in the air and his voice had a melodic tone to it. In harmony, the entire staff behind the counter as well as the staff performing duties in front of the counter sung back in chorus. "ONE 77 SPECIAL!"

Bill was afraid to ask. No he was embarrassed to ask, but he asked, "What is a 77 special?"

"Funny you should ask." Jonathan said as he went to actually make the 77 Special for Bill. Another staff member took over Jonathan's duties at the front till.

"Since time began there have been a select group of people who got it." Jonathan started. "And a select group of people who did not get it."

"Am I one of the one's who does not get it?"

Jonathan let that question sit a while as he started to prepare the drink. He used a blender and started to place ingredients into it on the fly.

"No. In fact there are things that you do get, that others do not and vice versa. All of life is set up to be an exchange between those who know something and those who want to know something, or those who have something and those who want to have something."

Bill started to say something in response, when Jonathan closed the blender lid and started the blender with a squealing roar.

When Jonathan stopped the blender, he spoke again, "By the way this 77 Special is paid for."

Bill was stunned, not by the free drink, just by the drink itself, and just before he lost his mind totally to the thought of it, he said, "Thanks."

"Enjoy."

"Okay."

"Go sit over there in that corner." Jonathan pointed to one corner of the coffee shop.

With a quick glance, the bright sunlight outside silhouetted every person and Bill could see that every table was taken.

"But?"

"I want you to meet Shirley."

Walking behind Jonathan, Bill could not see Shirley as they moved forward. Jonathan walked towards the corner table and then moved to one side. Immediately, Bill recognized that Shirley was a mature woman, healthy and wealthy looking, and with a broad welcoming smile. She held a 77 Special in her hand.

On the table, Jonathan set down two ice filled old style Coca-Cola glasses and two fresh bottles of Evian spring water that sparkled in the sun.

"Bill Right." Jonathan started, "Meet, Shirley Rich."

Bill took this all in. Shirley Rich. Mature woman. Late sixties, early seventies, or seventy-seven, he had never been very good at guessing a person's age.

"Hello." Bill said holding out his hand, "It's my pleasure."

"The pleasure is about to begin." Shirley smiled.

Jonathan backed away while saying, "I'll leave you to it."

"Please sit." Shirley continued.

Bill sat down. He had yet to take a drink of his 77 Special.

"I hope you love it." Shirley said.

"I'm not too sure about it."

"It's my recipe, it really puts fire in my day."

"Fire?"

"Passion would be more accurate. And seeing as Jonathan hooked you up with a 77

Special, it would appear that he thinks you need some more passion in your life."

Shirley held up her 77 Special, "Cheers!"

"Cheers." Bill said and watched Shirley savor her drink in tasty mouthfuls.

She smiled.

Bill took his first sip and was hit by sweet passion fruit with some strawberry. Next, the cayenne pepper and lemon kicked in, and he breathed in deeply through his nose. Finally, the ice and half and half cream soothed his pallette. A smile crossed his face.

"I like it."

"Good."

"No really. I like it."

"That is good." Shirley patted Bill's

arm, "So do you know why you are here?"

"Jonathan brought me over."

"No. I mean - *why you are here*?"

"No."

"Why do you think you are here?"

"I guess ..."

"Guessing is okay, but knowing is better." Shirley interrupted. "Let me start this from a different tact."

"Okay."

"Tell me what you said to Jonathan, that made him give you a 77 Special."

"Well, I was wrapped up in my thoughts when I came in. Jonathan asked me ... I remember now, Jonathan asked me 'What's it going to take?', and I thought that's the question right there, 'what's it going to take to make it this year?'"

"Make what?"

"Financial freedom for my family."

"How far along are you on that journey?"

"Pretty good I think. I'm currently in a good job. It pays the bills and gives us stability and we have home and life insurance and we even have some bonus money each year that goes into Retirement savings."

"That sounds like you have some financial freedom already."

"I guess you're right. I know friends who are worse off than our family."

"So what does this financial freedom you want look like?"

"No daily job. Enough money to live off of without ever hardly working."

"Bill, do you know the definition of the word 'work'?"

"Well I guess so."

"What is it?"

"Work is a nine to five daily grind. I really don't want that daily grind which also puts the majority of money into someone else's pocket."

Shirley let the silence between them grow and then she said, "Work is physical and mental effort directed towards a definite goal. Even when you are financially free, you are going to work. When things change, you will set new goals and work towards them."

"I can see that."

"Plus you are going to want to keep

working or you will get bored and die. If you are hardly working then whatever you put into place will also be hardly working for you."

Shirley paused for effect, then went on. "Do you think Oprah Winfrey hardly works? Or Bill Gates? Or Warren Buffett?"

"Well I never really thought of it. I think they work, but they do things they love."

"Do you think that is all they do, work at things they love?"

Bill thought about this deeper. "No. They probably had to work through things they didn't love too."

"Exactly." Shirley smiled, "They had to work through things they didn't love in order to create the things they do love. Can you see the difference?"

"I think so." Bill said.

"You would love to create Financial Freedom, is that right?"

Bill nodded.

"In order to get there, you may have to do some things that you do not love in order to create what you do love."

Bill nodded.

"So in some respect the things you do not love, you are going to have to love enough in order to get to the things you really love."

Bill thought about this out loud, "... to love enough to get through them, or love enough to change them."

"Rarely can we change the outer circumstances and events. What you are really going to be loving is yourself and your ability to get from where you are to where you want to be."

Bill took another sip of his 77 Special and looked outside. He thought about loving himself more and trying to change himself in order to get from where he was to where he wanted to be.

Shirley finished her 77 Special and waited for Bill to talk again.

Bill finally asked, "So what's it going to take?"

"That's the question, but before you answer it let's talk about Napoleon Hill."

"Napoleon Hill?"

"Napoleon Hill is best known for the book *Think and Grow Rich*. Have you ever read it?"

"Years ago, but I don't really remember it."

"That's okay. I first read *Think and*

Grow Rich in 1977. It was a special year. 77. Special." Shirley laughed. "It was in that year that I discovered the principles that have transformed my life."

"What are they?" Bill asked.

"At the end of Napoleon Hill's life, he was asked, 'which of all the principles he had shared was the most important one' and he replied, 'there are two, you must have a Definite Major Purpose and a Burning Desire.'"

Bill smiled, "Do I have them?"

"Before I answer that, let me describe them in a little more detail. It took Napoleon Hill twenty-five years to compile the information for his book, *Think and Grow Rich*. He did this through interviewing some of the most successful men of his or any time for that matter. Napoleon Hill wrote that 98% of the world thinks that a Definite Major Purpose is to HAVE FUN or to HAVE MORE

MONEY. Napoleon Hill also said that only about 2% of the world has a Definite Major Purpose written down and that they go on to achieve it. So I ask you, Bill Right, **'Have you written down your Definite Major Purpose?'**

"No."

"Well then, the author of *Alice's Adventures in Wonderland*, Lewis Carroll wrote, "If you don't know where you are going, any road will get you there."

"But I know where I am going. I am going to Financial Freedom."

"You think so. Tell me what are your exact monthly income and expenses right now?"

"I don't know. I haven't written them down."

"What are your monthly income and

expenses going to be when you are Financially Free?"

"I don't know."

"If you don't know where you are going, any road will get you there."

Bill sat there thinking. Shirley had presented a whole bunch of ideas to him with an intensity that surprised Bill.

"Before you say anything else," Shirley continued, "I will just tell you that you have the potential to achieve whatever you desire, but you will have to work to make it a reality. I can set you onto the path, but you will have to do the work."

Bill listened.

"If you are serious about this, you will have to do some homework. Once the homework is complete you will have to meet me again."

"I can do that."

"Bill, this is not to be taken lightly. Napoleon Hill also said that only 2% of the world puts these things into motion. That means that 98% of the world does not. Most people are not willing to do the work that will be required. It doesn't have to be hard, but you will have to be passionate. So ask yourself, are you sure you want to give up most of your social life, risk alienating friends and family, and be viewed as someone with a crazy vision? Is this something that is really worth it for you?"

Bill sat quietly thinking about everything Shirley had just shared. Give up things? Alienating others? Crazy? Is it worth it? Enough people already thought he was crazy. What would be nice, is if he really had something to show for it.

Shirley looked at Bill and said, "So what's it going to take to make it this year?"

"A Definite Major Purpose and my Passion to keep going no matter what comes to me."

"That's a good start." Shirley said, "And you are going to have to do your homework."

Shirley reached into her purse, pulled out two white invitation sized envelops , and then pushed them across the table to Bill. Clearly marked on them were #1 and #2.

"Until you have completed #1 don't bother opening #2." Shirley said. "Remember the more you put into this, the more you will get out of this."

Shirley stood up and held her hand out to Bill, "The pleasure has been all mine Bill. I wish you continued success in whatever you choose."

They shook hands and then Shirley walked down the street into the sun filled morning.

ENVELOP #1

Bill sat in the coffee shop and stared at the two envelopes. Thoughts rushed through his mind. He knew very little about Shirley Rich but he felt an immediate connection to what she had said. And he trusted Jonathan's opinion. Bill and he were only coffee shop acquaintances, but Bill always felt that Jonathan was a hard working straight shooting person.

Envelop #1 glowed in front of him.

Did he have what it would take? Was he in the 2%? In school he had not been. In college he had not been. However, was being in the top 2% in school the same thing?

Bill thought he had a Definite Major Purpose in wanting Financial Freedom. He also believed he had a Burning Desire that could instill enough love in himself to move forward through the obstacles that would stand between him and his desires.

Envelop #1 beaconed.

Bill picked up envelop #1 and was about to open it when he had a sensation of being watched and he looked around the coffee shop tables.

Everyone was in their own coffee drinking conversations, or newspaper reading, or Internet surfing worlds.

Bill grabbed the two envelopes and proceeded towards the front door and shouted in to Jonathan, "Thanks"

"You're welcome." Jonathan replied.

Bill felt different, this whole experience helped him get into a different place. Worries that seemed so troublesome when he walked into the coffee shop this morning were all but forgotten now.

Outside in the sunlight, Jonathan walked and opened envelop #1 and read the hand written letter that he pulled out.

Welcome to the first day of the rest of your life.

No matter what you have, or have not done up until now you can change your actions in order to create your desired results.

Here is the homework you need to accomplish before you open envelop #2:

You must define where you are right now as clearly as you can and where you want to go in the following areas.

1.   Physical
2.   Mental
3.   Emotional
4.   Spiritual
5.   Financial
6.   Relationships
7.   World Contribution

Because we already talked about the clarity of financial income and expenses, I think you will understand the exactness of this assignment. The more you put into it, the more you will get out of it.

Take as much time as you need to do this but set a due date for yourself so as that you actually get it done. By the way, one week is about 2% of a year. Please use this information to inspire, not deter.

When you have clearly defined these areas of your life, then and only then open and read the contents of envelop #2.

That seemed easy enough. Just clearly define where you are right now, and where you want to go. Bill knew he could do that and he set a time frame. Bill thought about the one week time line. He would have to do this exercise in his free time, no television or movie watching this week. He could do that. No, he would do that. He made a commitment to himself to do it.

Bill bought a journal, and over the next few lunch hours and nights he wrote down as clearly as he could, where he was and where he wanted to be in the seven areas. On the next two pages is a snapshot of his answers.

Physical Now: I am healthy. I take time to relax and rejuvenate. I eat a lot of junk food when watching movies. I take . . .

Physical Goals: I would like to be working out on a regular basis. I prepare healthy snacks to eat while watching movies. . .

Mental Now: I read about one book a year. I watch science programs. I have always wanted to learn a new language . . .

Mental Goals: I read one book a month. I take a foreign language class. I teach a class in the community . . .

Emotional Now: I get angry with my co-workers, customers, kids, and spouse sometimes . . .

Emotional Goals: I learn and use skills to deal with my emotions. I take time to love and support myself and others.

Spiritual Now: I do not belong to any religious group. I believe in the goodness of life and people, but I am not really sure what that is exactly.. . .

Spiritual Goals: I have a clear understanding of my place and purpose in the world. My confidence and calmness inspires others . . .

Financial Now: I have $ X in consumer debt. My monthly income is $ Y and expenses are $ Z . . .

Financial Goals: I am Financially Free. I have no consumer debt. My monthly income is $ $4Y$ and expenses are $ Z . . .

Relationships Now: I could spend more time with my spouse and family. I complain about the kids rather than praise them . . .

Relationships Goals: I praise everyone first and foremost. I spend time making our family environment healthy and happy . . .

World Contribution Now: Very little . . .

World Contribution Goals: If I were totally free, I could contribute in many different and fun ways I would . . .

ENVELOP #2

Bill was very satisfied with the work he had put into his answers. Once he actually sat down and did it, it ended up being less work than he feared before he had started.

In his home office he had tacked up envelop #2 on the cork board beside his desk as a carrot to keep him moving forward.

Now that he was done the work of envelop #1, he took a deep breath and said to himself, "Good work." He sat there basking in the feelings of a job well done. Then he looked over at envelop #2 and wondered, what it would say inside?

He walked over, opened it and read.

All the things you have written down about where you are and where you want to be are all part of the inner game of life. The inner game is about to become an important part of your life.

To learn more about the inner game, please come prepared to Volunteer on the next Thursday afternoon from 4 pm to 8 pm at the Children's Hospital. I'll meet you at the East Main Doors at 3:50.

CHILDREN'S HOSPITAL

Bill arrived early, and right at 3:50 Shirley came from inside the hospital to greet him, "Hello Bill."

"Hello Shirley."

"I guess you put some work in."

"I did."

"Are you clearer now?"

"Definitely."

"Are you ready to get some crystal clarity?"

"Yeah."

"Follow me."

Shirley walked into the Hospital. Bill followed behind her.

"So you want to know more about the inner game I bet."

"Yes I do."

"Before we get there, what do you think the inner game is about?"

"Well, because the note said that everything I had already done was a part of the inner game, I was thinking that the inner game had to do with my beliefs and perceptions about life."

"That's very good. Not everyone gets that. They get it, but they don't always understand it."

Shirley opened and stepped through a door that said, *Volunteer Office*. Inside,

Shirley spoke to the woman seated behind a desk, "This is Bill Right. He is going to help us this week."

"Wonderful."

For the next four hours, Shirley and Bill helped with whatever activities were needed. Bill did not love all of the activities, and he saw some things at the hospital that were disheartening to him, but mostly he felt a sense of connection with Shirley and the children and the other members of the Children's Hospital staff that he had not expected before he started.

When they were done, Shirley asked Bill, "So what did you learn about the inner game?"

"I am not sure."

"What did you remember about yourself as you volunteered?"

"I had more fun than I thought I would."

"Fun, that's one key."

"I was helping others."

"Helping others, that's another key."

"I'm not too proud of it, but a lot of times I thought and felt things I didn't want to when I saw some of the kids."

"Listening to your feelings, that's another key."

"And you know, I never would have said this, but there was a lot of good things going on here. I always think of hospitals as dreary places. I don't know what it was, but there is a lot of good here."

"Praising God/Life/Energy, that's the forth key." Shirley said, "You got all of the inner game keys."

"What were they exactly?" Bill asked

"#1 Praise God/Life/Energy.

"#2 Have fun.

"#3 Help Others.

"#4 Listen to your feelings.

"Together those are the four keys of the inner game."

"I don't think I understand them all."

"Let's go for coffee in the cafeteria. We'll find your understanding there."

In the cafeteria, seated and enjoying coffee, Shirley continued, "Success in everything is a combination of two effective aspects. Effective Beliefs which make up the inner game, and Effective Actions which make up the outer game.

"Why so many people fail in life is that they have ineffective beliefs or ineffective actions and when they do not achieve what they want, they quit because they believe they cannot get there or their actions take them away from where they say they want to go.

"So let me explain the four inner game keys in a way you can understand and remember them."

"I'd love that."

"Actually, you are going to explain them to me."

"What?"

"I'll help by giving you the key, and then you are going to explain it to me."

"Okay. What was the first one again?"

"#1 Praise God/Life/Energy."

"Praise God/Life/Energy. I said that I was surprised about how much good there was in the hospital, and you said that was the key. I think what you are saying is that I found the good that was there and focused on that, but what exactly do you mean by God/Life/Energy?"

"I just say, God/Life/Energy because there are so many ways you could describe the All That Is. You could call it the Universe or Charlie or the Unmanifested Manifested.

"It was Albert Einstein who said, 'the most fundamental question we can ask is: is the universe a friendly place?' Until you see the universe as a friendly place, you will see the universe as an unfriendly place. When you see the universe as unfriendly, you will go around cursing things rather than praising them.

"The sooner you Praise God/Life/Energy or whatever you choose to call it, the sooner you will discover that the universe is really set up to have everyone win."

"I think I see what you are saying. I don't really think of God as you are describing God."

"Then don't say God, just say Life. The sooner you Praise Life, and the people, places, things, and experiences you meet in Life, the sooner your inner game supports the creation of your dreams.

"Now, #2 was Have Fun." Shirley said.

"I think this one goes back to what you said on the first day we met. You have to love what you are doing. It may not be what you want to do, but it is what you are doing, and it is leading you to what you want to do. If you can make the way you approach everything fun, then it will be a fun journey to the more fun you imagine."

"Sounds great." Shirley said, "#3 was Help Others."

"I think that when we are helping others we get out of our own way. We get so wrapped up in wanting things for ourselves. I have to admit that when I opened the second envelop I was disappointed to read that I would be volunteering at a Children's Hospital. I said to myself, 'how is that going to teach me about being Financially Free?' Now I realize I have so much Financial Freedom already that I can easily help others. It's not like I am one of these people who is working three jobs to make ends meet."

"Very good, and #4 Listen to your feelings"

" I need help with this one. This one has me baffled."

"Most people do." Shirley said, "Have you ever heard of the authors Esther and Jerry Hicks?"

"No."

"For over twenty years now they have been sharing a message about listening to your feelings. The very basis of their message is that if you feel good you are moving towards your dreams, while if you feel bad you are moving away from your dreams."

"Okay."

"Here is how it works in practical terms. First you need a clearly defined goal."

"I wrote mine down."

"That's very important. When you have a clearly defined goal that is written down and you think about yourself as moving successfully towards it, you feel good. When I say good, you could be feeling excited, or joyous, or any way that feels good.

"When you have this same goal and you think about yourself as not achieving it, you feel bad. When I say bad, you could be angry, or depressed, or frustrated, or any way that feels bad. Do you understand this?"

"I think so. I write down my clearly defined goal and when I think it is coming, I will feel good, but when I think it is not, I feel bad, is that it?"

"Yes. Now even more important is to recognize that it is only your thoughts that ever make you feel bad, not what others may do in your experience. This is where many people lose their way when they are following their feelings. Let me be more specific."

"Go for it."

"Let's say your clearly defined written down goal is to create $5,000 a month in passive income for Financial Freedom."

"Okay."

"Let's say that a friend or family member says to you, 'How in the world do you expect to achieve $5,000 a month for

Financial Freedom, when you can't even keep a regular job.'"

"Got it."

"Now when they say that, you feel bad. Now I ask you, 'why do you feel bad?'"

"I feel bad because they don't believe in my dreams, and maybe at some level what they say has some truth to it."

"Wrong."

"Wrong?"

"The only reason you ever feel bad is because your thoughts do not see you as successfully reaching your goal."

"Can you explain that?"

"Definitely. Your goal is $5,000 a month for Financial Freedom. Your friend or family member can say anything they want, but if you *think*, you are going to reach your goal of $5,000 a month, you will feel good no matter what someone else says. And you will do whatever it takes to make your dream a reality. Similarly if you *think*, you can't make it, you will feel bad, and won't do what it takes to make it."

"Is that delusional?"

Shirley laughed, "It can be if all you are doing is working on your inner game. However when you have both your inner game and your outer game working together, it will be Incredible."

"How so?"

"That's the next lesson."

"When do I take that lesson?"

"This Saturday."

"Great!"

"I'll meet you at Jonathan's Coffee Shop at 7am."

"7am." Bill breathed in deeply until he realized his thoughts were taking him away from where he wanted to go. "I'll be there."

SATURDAY MORNING

Bill arrived early at Jonathan's Coffee Shop. He was going to order two 77 Specials, but Shirley already had them in her hands when he walked up at 6:45.

"Morning." Shirley smiled and held out a 77 Special.

"Morning. Thanks." Bill said taking the drink and gulping back an energizing mouthful.

"Excited?"

"Yeah, I am."

"Good. Today we are going to learn the Effective Actions of the outer game."

"Sounds great!"

"I'll drive." Shirley said.

"Where to?"

"A craft sale."

"Seriously?"

"Oh yeah."

When they got to Shirley's Car, Bill saw that it was full of kids and crafts.

They drove to a local school where a whole bunch of people were unloading their kids and crafts.

Bill's thoughts were far from his goals. He took a sip of his 77 Special and felt it's energy hit him. When the car had stopped, Bill said, "Let's have fun."

"Now you're getting it." Shirley said.

The day went by in a blur. At the craft fair, Bill and Shirley acted as managers for the kids and their crafts. By the end of the fair, almost 90% of their crafts were sold. After they had dropped the last of the kids and their crafts off at their respective homes, Shirley asked, "Do you have the time to go out to dinner?"

"Yes."

"It's my treat."

"Thank you."

At a small family run Italian restaurant, the owner greeted Shirley with joy.

"Shirley! Welcome. It is so good to see you."

"Thanks, Giuseppe."

"Who's this young man?"

"Giuseppe, meet Bill."

"It's a pleasure, Bill."

After they had sat down, Shirley ordered, "Two dinner specials, Giuseppe."

"Benissimo." Giuseppe left in a flourish.

Shirley said, "What did you learn about the outer game, Bill?"

"Set goals. Take action. Have fun. After that I'm not too sure."

"Not bad. I'll give them to you. You have to explain them to me."

"Fair enough."

"#1 Set Goals."

"You need a clearly defined goal. You explained to the kids today that goals are dreams with time lines. We had a goal to sell a certain number of crafts by lunch. We wrote it down as a team."

"Exactly."

"Also on our goal page, we wrote down our actions."

"That's #2 Take Action."

"You asked each kid to smile. You asked each kid to ask the people to look at the crafts they actually made. You asked each kid to ask for a sale."

"That's for sure. Each day you need to take actions that actually make you money otherwise you will be quickly out of business."

"Now I'm not sure what is next."

"#3 Get Feedback."

"Get feedback. Let's see. The kids . . .

the kids . . . I'm not sure."

"This one is a little harder to see. Do you remember when Julie was sad?"

"Oh yeah. I helped her get back on track. I told her some people may not want her product, but that doesn't mean it was because she made it."

"Precisely. One of the biggest mistakes people make is that they take rejection personally. Rejection in the form of feedback is the greatest opportunity to improve your product or service, when you actually listen to what people are saying about your product or service.

"Too many products get made each year and people spend a lot of money without ever getting any feedback at all and then they get no sales."

"I have seen that happen before."

"Me too, and #4 Evaluate and Set New Goals."

"At lunch we looked at our sales, everyone shared their feedback, and we changed out strategy and set new goals based on our feedback. With our new action steps in the afternoon, we went on to sell almost all of our product."

"Wasn't it great?"

"Yeah, we didn't even drop the price. We just packaged a few things together. All of a sudden our products had a higher value in people's minds and bam! Sales explosion!"

Shirley laughed, "Now you get the concepts of the effective inner and outer games."

"Is it really that easy?"

"The concepts are simple, and the execution can be fun, but rarely does it come easy. You are really going to have to work to make these ideas work for you."

"I can see that."

"Life is not just a kids' craft fair."

Bill laughed, "Thank God!"

They had a wonderful dinner and talked about many things, covering the many aspects of physical, mental, emotional, spiritual, financial, relationship, and world contribution freedoms. At the end of dinner, Bill asked, "So now what do I do?"

Shirley pulled from her purse one white invitation envelope with #3 on it and a large manilla envelop with the #4 on it.

"You may open #3 right now."

Bill opened it and read the following note.

ENVELOP #3

Effective Beliefs and Effective Actions Create an Effective Game.

Work is physical (outer game) and mental (inner game) efforts directed towards a definite (written down) goal.

What's it going to take?

1. A Definite Major Purpose clearly defined and written down.
2. A Burning Desire to achieve it when things get rough.

Inner Game
1. Praise God/Life/Energy. See the Universe as a Friendly Place helping everyone to win.
2. Have Fun. It may not be what you want to do, but it is what you are doing until you get to do what you want to do, so Have Fun.

3. Help Others: If your product/service Helps Others by making our world a better place, you will become very rich for your Help.

4. Listen to Your Feelings: Bad Feelings mean your ineffective thoughts are taking you away from the fulfillment of your dreams. Good Feelings mean your Effective thoughts are taking you towards the fulfilment of your dreams.

Outer Game

1. Set Goals: Dreams with deadlines.

2. Take Action: Fun Money Making Daily Actions.

3. Get Feedback: Listen to what people say about your product.

4. Evaluate and Set New Goals: Keep working and you will make it.

After Bill finished reading, Shirley said, "That's a compilation of what we've remembered together. As to what's in envelop #4, there's a book. This book is not for everyone. So many people think that making a lot of money is easy when they have never made a lot of money before.

"If you want to learn more on this journey, this book will encourage you to start small and build from there. How can you make $10,000 a month in passive income tomorrow, when you don't even make $10 a month in passive income today?

"Only open envelop #4 if you are really prepared to put in the work. You do remember what the definition of work was, don't you?"

Bill nodded, "Work is physical and mental effort directed towards a definite goal."

"Most people are not ready or willing to do the work. Napoleon Hill said that a mere 2% of the people in the world do. I believe that everyone has the potential, but only you can believe and work your potential. No one else is going to do it for you."

ENVELOP #4

The contents of envelop #4 are found within:

**I AM Creating My Own
Financial Freedom: The Lessons**

ISBN 978-0-9813485-3-7

77 Special Recipe
by
Binah C Godisall

Serves 1

1/2 cup passion fruit juice
6 large sweet strawberries
1/8 tsp cayenne pepper
1/8 tsp lemon zest
1/2 cup ice
1/4 cup cream

Place fruit in blender with spice and lemon zest.
Blend until smooth.
Pour over ice (crushed and cube)
Top with cream.
Add straw and serve.

ABOUT THE AUTHOR

Barry Thomas Bechta is an artist, author, and film maker whose work centers around the concepts of Unconditional Love. Barry knew he wanted to write from a very young age and was encouraged with his artistic skills and only began writing full time in his thirties. He wrote his first book, *I AM Creating My Own Experience* as a personal journal to choose connection with God/Life/Energy. He has since written 17 inspirational books.

Barry loves to hear from people whom have connected with his writing and used it as a tool to improve their lives. If you would like to write him about your personal experiences as a result of reading any of his books, Barry encourages you to do so.

You can also get a Free Digital Copy of *I AM Creating My Own Experience - The Creation Vibration* from his main website:

www.unconditionallovebooks.com

All of the above are books are available through your local
bookstore, or they may be ordered as digital downloads at
www.unconditionallovebooks.com

Barry Thomas Bechta is available for interviews, special events, workshops, and lectures that redefine, guide, and inspire everyone's connection to the Creative Power within themselves. To arrange author interviews, special events, workshops, or lectures, please contact:

**UNCONDITIONAL
LOVE BOOKS**

**Unconditional Love Books
Box # 610 - 2527 Pine St.,
Vancouver, BC, Canada V6J 3E8**

info@unconditionallovebooks.com

www.unconditionallovebooks.com

For additional copies of Barry's books, products, and services please contact your local book seller. Many products and services are Only available to order directly from the publisher as eProducts on the website.

Thanks for your purchase and Remember to Consciously Create your Life.

**Right Now is the Only Moment of Creation
Enjoy it Fully!**

www.ingramcontent.com/pod-product-compliance
Lightning Source LLC
Chambersburg PA
CBHW032015190326
41520CB00007B/480